Young Woman and the Sea

The Inspiring True Story of Trudy Ederle's Triumph Over the English Channel

Harper Blackwood

Copyright

Disclaimer

This non-fiction book, titled "Young Woman and the Sea: The Inspiring True Story of Trudy Ederle's Triumph Over the English Channel," is based on historical events and Trudy Ederle's life. While every effort has been taken to accurately depict the facts and events, some information may have been interpreted or contextualized for narrative reasons. The ideas and interpretations stated in this book are the author's and may not reflect the opinions or beliefs of all those concerned. Readers are advised to examine supplementary sources for a more complete knowledge of the subject matter.

Table Of Contents

Introduction

Gertrude Ederle, a name synonymous with unwavering resolve and pioneering energy, has a unique position in history. Her narrative, as told in "Young Woman and the Sea," is about more than simply her astounding accomplishment of swimming across the English Channel; it is also about the broader consequences of her achievements in breaking down societal barriers and confronting gender stereotypes. Ederle was born on October 23, 1905, in New York City, as the third of six children in a German immigrant family. She had a natural passion for water from a young age, and she spent many days at the beach perfecting her swimming skills. Her family's encouragement, combined with her own desire, inspired her to pursue competitive swimming, a sport dominated by men at the time.

Ederle's early success in competitive swimming was a reflection of her talent and hard effort. She broke several records, including a world record in the 800-meter freestyle at the age of 17. Her swimming abilities immediately earned her notoriety, and she represented the United States at the 1924 Summer Olympics in Paris, where she won three medals: one gold in the 4x100 meter freestyle relay and two bronze medals in solo freestyle events. These accomplishments were impressive, but they were merely a prelude to the huge task she would shortly face.

The English Channel, a body of water that spans approximately 21 miles between England and France, has long been a prize for long-distance swimmers. At the time, the Channel had only been successfully crossed a few times, all by men. Despite the intimidating scenario, Ederle remained unfazed. She regarded the Channel as both a personal challenge and an opportunity to showcase women's athletic talents. In the 1920s, cultural expectations for women were primarily limited, with sports and physical effort considered inappropriate for women. Ederle's desire to conquer the Channel was as much about defying prejudices as it was about setting a record.

In 1925, Ederle made her first attempt to swim the Channel. Despite intense training and preparation, the attempt failed. After nine hours in the sea, Ederle was rescued by her coach, who cited safety concerns. This failure, however, only strengthened her resolve. Ederle returned to the United States and resumed her training with fresh vigor. She developed her technique, increased her endurance, and studied the Channel's currents and tides. The next year, on August 6, 1926, she returned to the Channel, determined to make history.

The conditions on the day of her swim were tough. The water was chilly, and the tides were powerful. Ederle donned a specially crafted silk bikini that she had covered with lanolin to keep warm. She sailed out from Cape Gris-Nez, France, with a support boat, aiming for the English coast. The trek was exhausting, with powerful currents frequently steering her off course. However, Ederle's training and mental strength saw her through. After 14 hours and 34 minutes in the ocean, she arrived at the shore of Kingsdown, England. She not only became the first woman to swim the English Channel, but she also broke the previous record by more than two hours, which was held by a man.

Ederle's victory was more than simply a personal one; it was a watershed moment that resonated far beyond the realm of sports. Her successful swim called into question long-held beliefs about women's physical limitations and demonstrated that women could compete at the top levels of endurance sports. Her accomplishment received widespread media coverage, and when she returned to the United States, she was hailed as a national hero. There were parades in her honor, and she was invited to see President Calvin Coolidge, who dubbed her "America's best girl."

Despite his accomplishments and popularity, Ederle remained humble and grounded. She frequently discussed the value of perseverance and the support she received from her family and coaches. Her victory motivated numerous women to pursue their own sporting goals and paved the way for future generations of female athletes. In the years that followed, Ederle remained active in swimming and worked as a swim instructor, sharing her enthusiasm and knowledge with others.

However, Ederle's life following the Channel Swim was not without difficulties. She sustained a significant back injury in a diving accident, limiting her ability to swim competitively. She also had to deal with the harsh realities of celebrity life, which can be overpowering at times. Despite these challenges, Ederle remained a strong figure, exemplifying the attitude of endurance and dedication that had distinguished her career.

When considering Gertrude Ederle's relevance, it is crucial to consider the broader implications of her accomplishments. Her swim across the English Channel was more than just a sporting achievement; it was a cultural and social milestone that shook the status quo and broadened women's opportunities in all disciplines. In an era when women were frequently limited to traditional roles and denied opportunities for self-expression and achievement, Ederle's success served as a striking message about what women could accomplish when given the opportunity.

Furthermore, Ederle's legacy goes beyond her record-breaking swim. She was an advocate for water safety and the benefits of swimming, particularly among young people. Her work as a swim instructor contributed to the sport's promotion and safety, allowing more people to enjoy the water. Ederle's life and achievements continue to inspire us, reminding us of the value of setting lofty objectives, working relentlessly to attain them, and smashing down barriers along the way.

The challenge of the English Channel swim

The English Channel, a 21-mile length of water connecting England's southern and northern coasts, has long served as a symbol of both challenge and achievement for swimmers. Its frigid seas, powerful currents, and unpredictable weather make it one of the most daunting natural obstacles on the planet. For generations, this narrow yet deadly strait has captivated the minds of adventurers and athletes alike, with everyone hoping to conquer its treacherous waters. Among these daring spirits was Gertrude Ederle, a young lady whose dedication and perseverance would not only allow her to cross the Channel, but also shatter cultural boundaries and create new sporting standards.

In the early twentieth century, the concept of a woman trying such a feat was regarded as daring, if not impossible. Since Captain Matthew Webb's initial crossing of the English Channel in 1875, only a few men had successfully completed the journey. The swim's physical demands were exceptional, requiring incredible endurance, strength, and mental fortitude. Swimmers feared temperatures as low as 50 degrees Fahrenheit, currents that might knock them off course, and waves that could rise abruptly. For women, who were frequently perceived as physically weaker and less capable, the Channel posed an even larger challenge—one that many feared could not be overcome.

Gertrude Ederle, a New York City native born in 1905, was unconcerned about these prevalent attitudes. Ederle, a gifted swimmer from an early age, had already established herself as a successful athlete by the time she decided to swim the Channel. She held several world records and competed in the 1924 Summer Olympics, winning a gold and two bronze medals. Her swimming abilities were evident, but the notion of swimming the English Channel was a new and terrifying task, requiring not only technique but also an extraordinary resolve to achieve.

Ederle's decision to try the Channel swim was motivated by a strong desire to demonstrate that women could perform the same physical accomplishments as men. She trained hard, spending hours every day in the water swimming large distances to improve her endurance and accustom her body to frigid temperatures. Her training was thorough, with an emphasis on both physical and mental preparedness. She practiced breathing techniques to conserve energy and keep a consistent speed, and she worked with a coach, Thomas Burgess, who had previously swum the Channel. Ederle also enlisted the assistance of a support crew, which included her father and sister, who would join her on the boat ride across the Channel.

The first attempt occurred on August 18, 1925. Ederle entered the water in Cape Gris-Nez, France, with the intention of reaching the English coastline. She donned a specially made swimsuit to avoid drag and greased her body to keep warm. Despite her diligent preparations, the swim proved difficult. Strong gusts and rough seas made travel slow and exhausting. Ederle battled the weather for more than eight hours before her coach, concerned for her safety, removed her from the ocean. She was devastated by the decision, believing that she was capable of finishing the swim. However, this setback just strengthened her resolve. Ederle returned to the United States, increased her training efforts, and resolved to try again.

One year later, on August 6, 1926, Gertrude Ederle attempted her second swim across the English Channel. This time, she was better prepared and more motivated than before. She began at the same location, Cape Gris-Nez, and faced the cold, rough waters of the Channel. The weather improved, but the swim remained a difficult effort. Ederle had to deal with surges up to several feet high, currents that threatened to drive her off course, and the constant cold that depleted her strength. She swam tirelessly, never slowing down and refusing to be discouraged by the conditions. Her support team stayed close by, offering encouragement and nutrition.

As the hours passed, it became evident that Ederle was on course to not only finish the swim, but also set a new record. She kept up a great speed, her powerful strokes pulling her forward despite the weariness and cold. Gertrude Ederle, the first woman to swim the English Channel, arrived in Kingsdown, England, after 14 hours and 34 minutes in the water. Her time was the fastest ever recorded, breaking the previous record set by a man by nearly two hours.

Ederle's success was remarkable, not only because she completed one of the world's most difficult swims, but also because she broke societal expectations and demonstrated that women could do extraordinary physical feats. Her achievement was lauded all around the world, and she became a symbol of tenacity and resilience. The media acclaimed her as the "Queen of the Waves," and she was greeted with parades and plaudits upon her return to the United States.

The significance of Gertrude Ederle's swim went far beyond athletics. It was a watershed moment for women's rights and gender equality, challenging preconceived preconceptions about what women might accomplish. Ederle's achievement motivated countless women and girls to pursue their own athletic goals, breaking down long-standing restrictions to women's involvement in competitive sports. Her narrative demonstrated the strength of tenacity and the value of defying the status quo.

In the years following her historic swim, Gertrude Ederle remained an advocate for women's athletics and an inspiration to many. She worked as a swimming instructor and utilized her celebrity to promote swimming and fitness. Although her hearing was impaired during the swim, resulting in partial deafness, Ederle never allowed it dampen her enthusiasm for the sport she loved. She remained a revered figure in the swimming community, as well as an enduring emblem of bravery and dedication.

Gertrude Ederle's swim across the English Channel is a triumph over adversity, a tribute to the human spirit, and a compelling reminder that with the correct mindset and commitment, no endeavor is impossible. Her legacy lives on through the innumerable women who have followed in her footsteps, overcoming obstacles and breaking down barriers in athletics and beyond. As we reflect on her incredible journey, we are reminded of the power of dreams and the perseverance of those who dare to achieve them.

Chapter One

Early Life and Passion for Swimming

Gertrude Ederle, aka "Trudy," was born on October 23, 1905, in New York City. She grew up in a family of six children, her parents being German immigrants. The Ederle family owned a butcher shop in Manhattan, offering a solid, albeit humble, upbringing. Gertrude's early existence was typical of the time, but her fate was far from ordinary. She had a natural affinity for water from a young age, which would shape her career and break down boundaries for women in sports.

Gertrude learned to swim as a child thanks to her father, who thought that every child should be able to swim for their own protection. The family spent the summers at their home in Highlands, New Jersey, where young Gertrude first witnessed the vastness of the ocean. Many others found the Atlantic's waves daunting, but Gertrude saw them as both a challenge and an opportunity. Her father recognized her excitement and taught her the fundamentals of swimming, instilling in her both talent and confidence. This initial encounter to water laid the groundwork for what would become a lifelong obsession.

Gertrude's passion in swimming developed swiftly into a serious hobby. She joined the local New York Women's Swimming Association, which played an important part in developing her talent. The club, formed by women for women, offered a welcoming environment for young female swimmers to practice and compete. At a time when women's sports were not commonly acknowledged or sponsored, this club provided Gertrude with the opportunity to hone her skills in a disciplined and welcoming environment.

Gertrude's potential began to flourish under the direction of her coach, former Olympic swimmer Louis de Breda Handley. Handley helped her refine her technique and encourage her to go beyond what she thought was possible. He saw her great natural talent, especially her endurance and strength, which were essential for long-distance swimming. Gertrude trained hard, spending hours in the water improving her strokes and increasing her stamina. Her determination was relentless, and she swiftly rose to the top of her age group's swimming rankings.

Gertrude was already achieving national records in swimming when she was 15 years old. She specialized in freestyle, excelling at both sprints and long distances. Her success in contests caught the attention of the national swimming community, and she was quickly regarded as a rising star. She competed in the National Women's Swimming Championships in 1921, at the age of 16, and took first place in numerous events, breaking new records and cementing her position as one of the country's top female swimmers.

Despite her accomplishments, Gertrude faced numerous hurdles. The 1920s were a time when traditional standards restricted what women could do, particularly in athletics. There considerable doubt regarding women's physical talents, and many thought that strenuous athletic activities were inappropriate for them. Swimming, especially in open water, was considered risky and unfeminine. Gertrude and her swimming association friends, on the other hand, challenged these prejudices, demonstrating that women can achieve in sports just as much as men do.

Gertrude's passion for swimming was not only about competition, but also about breaking new territory. She aspired to accomplish tasks that no woman had ever done before, and swimming across the English Channel was one of her most ambitious goals. The Channel, a 21-mile length of chilly, turbulent water connecting England and France, had long been regarded as one of the most difficult swims in the world. By the 1920s, only a few males had successfully completed the crossing, and no woman had ever tried. For

Gertrude, this was the ultimate challenge, a chance to demonstrate that women could perform great athletic feats.

Gertrude needed to polish her talents and increase her endurance in order to take on such a challenge. Her training program became even more intensive, with a concentration on long-distance swims and increasing her resistance to the cold. She exercised in numerous bodies of water, including lakes and the ocean, to become accustomed to varying conditions. Her coach, Handley, was an important part of her preparation, pushing her to her boundaries while also offering the technical expertise she need to enhance her efficiency and speed.

In addition to physical preparation, Gertrude needed to psychologically prepare for the upcoming task. Swimming the Channel needed not just physical stamina, but also enormous mental strength. Swimming in open water can be isolating, especially under difficult weather. Gertrude employed visualization techniques to increase her mental power, visualizing herself completing the swim and overcoming hurdles along the way. She was also inspired by her supporters and the growing number of women in athletics who were challenging traditional norms.

Gertrude Ederle was not only a good swimmer when she was ready to try the Channel swim; she was also a symbol of tenacity and women's athletic potential. Her journey from a small girl splashing in the waves to an elite athlete highlighted her dedication and passion. She had proven herself in several events, setting records and receiving awards, but the Channel swim symbolized something more significant. It was an opportunity to make history and challenge the world's expectations of what women could do.

Gertrude attempted to swim the English Channel for the first time in the summer of 1925. Despite her preparedness, the endeavor failed; bad weather and powerful currents compelled her to halt. Despite this setback, she remained determined. Instead, it reinforced her determination to succeed. Gertrude saw the failure as an opportunity to learn, rather than a defeat. She returned to her training with fresh zeal, ready to overcome the challenges that had held her back the first time.

One year later, on August 6, 1926, Gertrude Ederle completed the historic swim across the

English Channel. She swam for 14 hours and 34 minutes despite strong seas and frigid conditions, becoming the first woman to complete the passage. She not only succeeded, but she also broke the previous record set by a male, proving once and for all that women are capable of remarkable athletic feats. Her triumph was celebrated around the world, and she quickly became an international superstar, dubbed "America's Best Girl."

Gertrude Ederle's early background and enthusiasm for swimming laid the groundwork for her outstanding accomplishments. Her journey was defined by a passion for the water, a ferocious ambition to succeed, and an unwavering dedication to tearing down obstacles. She not only changed the face of swimming, but also had a tremendous impact on the overall landscape of women's sports. Gertrude Ederle became a pioneer thanks to her endurance and determination, paving the way for future generations of female athletes and motivating numerous others to pursue their aspirations despite societal expectations. Her narrative, as told in "Young Woman and the Sea," is a stunning monument to women's courage and fortitude in the face of hardship.

Chapter Two

The English Channel Challenge

The English Channel, a short body of water that separates England from continental Europe, has long posed a tough obstacle to swimmers. Its hazardous seas, unpredictable weather, and powerful currents have made it a symbol of fortitude and bravery. For Gertrude Ederle, a young woman who loves to swim, this endeavor was more than just a personal test; it was a statement about breaking down barriers. Her mission to cross the English Channel was defined by rigorous preparation, physical and mental fortitude, and an unwavering pursuit of a dream that appeared unachievable for women at the time.

Gertrude Ederle's passion with swimming began as a child growing up in New York City. Her father introduced her to swimming because he believed it had health benefits. Ederle immediately exhibited natural talent and a love of the water, prompting her to pursue competitive swimming. By the time she was a teenager, she had already broken multiple records and won several national championships, establishing herself as one of the top swimmers in the United States.

Even the most experienced swimmers found it difficult to complete the English Channel swim. The distance of around 21 miles may appear feasible, but the weather made it a whole different challenge. The frigid water, which may drop to 50°F (10°C), posed a serious risk of hypothermia. The strong tides and currents could easily knock swimmers off course, sometimes tripling the distance they had to cover. Furthermore, unpredictable weather can transform a serene sea into a rough, wave-tossed obstacle course in minutes.

Despite these hurdles, a few individuals had successfully swum the English Channel before to Ederle's effort. Captain Matthew Webb conducted the first successful swim across the channel in 1875, taking little under 22 hours. For decades, Webb's achievement served as a tribute to the remarkable stamina and perseverance required to cross the Channel. Women, on the other hand, have yet to achieve this achievement, owing to social beliefs of physical limitations and a lack of opportunity in competitive sports.

Gertrude Ederle was undeterred by these perceptions. Her determination to swim the

English Channel stemmed from a desire to demonstrate that women could do great things in sports, which were traditionally dominated by males. Ederle began her preparations with a strenuous training regimen that included long-distance ocean swims to help her body adjust to the cold water and difficult circumstances she would confront. Her training also concentrated on increasing stamina and muscle, which are necessary for enduring the lengthy hours of swimming required to cross the channel.

In addition to physical training, Ederle had to think about the technical components of the swim. She collaborated with her instructor, Jabez Wolffe, a seasoned Channel swimmer, to determine the best route and tactics for dealing with tides and currents. Ederle chose the

American crawl, sometimes known as freestyle, which was faster but required more energy than the breaststroke, the stroke normally employed by Channel swimmers. This decision was essential because it allowed her to travel faster through the water, decreasing her exposure to the cold.

Gertrude Ederle set out from Cape Gris-Nez, France, on August 6, 1926, accompanied by her coach and father aboard a boat. The beginning was fortunate, with calm seas and pleasant weather. However, as she progressed, the swim grew increasingly difficult in terms of endurance and resolve. Despite her preparation and protective coating of grease, the cold water penetrated into her muscles and caused cramps. The tides and currents proved unpredictable, sending her off track several times.

Nonetheless, Ederle's determination never faltered. She swam steadily, keeping her rhythm and pace despite the difficulties. Her support staff was vital in supplying her with sustenance and encouragement. They communicated with her via a sequence of hand gestures because speaking would waste valuable energy and time. Ederle's determination was challenged further when she faced a storm halfway through the swim. The waves grew rougher, and visibility dropped, making it impossible for her to stay on course.

Throughout these obstacles, Ederle shown exceptional mental fortitude. She concentrated on her aim, dividing the swim into smaller, more doable sections. This psychological method enabled her to retain her focus and avoid becoming overwhelmed by the size of the undertaking. As the hours passed, she kept pushing forward, her strokes solid and steadfast.

After 14 hours and 34 minutes in the ocean, Gertrude Ederle arrived at the shores of Kingsdown, England. She not only became the first woman to swim the English Channel, but she also broke the men's record by over two hours. Her achievement was lauded around the world as a triumph of the human spirit and perseverance. Ederle's accomplishment challenged long-held preconceptions about women's physical talents, paving the way for subsequent generations of female athletes.

Ederle's swim was more than just a personal achievement; it was also a cultural milestone. During a period when women were fighting for their rights and recognition in a variety of industries, her accomplishment stood out as a symbol of empowerment and opportunity. Her swim received widespread media coverage, propelling her to international celebrity status. Ederle's achievement encouraged countless women to pursue their aspirations despite societal expectations or limits.

Following her historic swim, Gertrude Ederle remained an advocate for women's athletics. She toured the United States, giving talks and demonstrations while actively advocating swimming and water safety. However, her competitive swimming career was cut short due to a back injury incurred in a car accident. Despite this loss, Ederle remained a popular person and an inspiration for endurance and tenacity.

Gertrude Ederle's narrative has been immortalized in novels and films, and it continues to inspire people today. Her swim across the English Channel is more than just a feat of athleticism; it's also a poignant story about tearing down barriers and confronting authority. Ederle's legacy continues on, reminding us of the value of courage, tenacity, and believing that with hard effort and perseverance, even the most difficult difficulties can be overcome.

When reflecting on Gertrude Ederle's achievements, it is critical to consider the overall context. Her triumphant swim across the English Channel was a watershed moment in sports history, proving that women could compete and achieve at the most difficult physical tasks. Ederle's voyage also demonstrated the value of support systems, as her family, coach, and crew all played crucial roles in her accomplishment. Her historic swim required a team effort as well as confidence in her skills.

Ederle's story also emphasizes the role of media in changing public perception and knowledge. The enormous coverage of her swim reached a global audience, inspiring many and sparking discussions about gender equality in sports. Her accomplishment was more than just a personal success; it was a collective triumph for women everywhere, breaking the norms and expectations of the day.

Gertrude Ederle is known today as a trailblazer, not only in swimming, but also in the larger context of women's rights and empowerment. Her legacy continues to inspire future generations of athletes and everyone who want to overcome difficulties and achieve their goals. Ederle's narrative demonstrates the strength of tenacity, the significance of breaking down barriers, and the lasting impact of individuals who dare to defy the odds.

As we celebrate the accomplishments of athletes and pioneers such as Gertrude Ederle, we must remember the context in which they lived and the hurdles they faced. Ederle's swim across the English Channel was more than just a physical feat; it was a daring statement against the constraints placed on women. Her strength and determination paved the path for future generations, allowing women to participate and be recognized more in sports.

In conclusion, Gertrude Ederle's remarkable swim across the English Channel remains a watershed moment in sporting history. It is a narrative of incredible bravery, persistence, and resilience, exemplifying the spirit of a real pioneer. Ederle's story is an inspiration to all, reminding us that with passion and determination, we can conquer even the most daunting problems. Her legacy lives on, inspiring us to push the limits of what is possible and to recognize the accomplishments of those who dare to dream large.

Chapter Three

The Historic Swim

The morning of August 6, 1926, began with a sense of expectation and uncertainty. The weather was not ideal, with turbulent seas and strong winds that would test even the most experienced swimmers. Gertrude Ederle, the young American woman standing on the French coast, remained unmoved. At only 20 years old, Ederle was about to make history as the first woman to swim across the English Channel, a feat previously accomplished by only five men. Her voyage was more than just a personal challenge; it also represented women's capabilities and determination.

Ederle has spent years preparing for this moment. She had already achieved several world records in competitive swimming, demonstrating her aquatic aptitude. Her preparation for the Channel swim was intense, with lengthy hours in cold water to accustom her body to the extreme temperatures she would encounter. She also worked on increasing her stamina, knowing that the swim may last anywhere from 10 to 20 hours. Ederle's confidence was matched by her thorough training, which included creating a unique swimming style that combined speed and energy conservation, allowing her to swim at a consistent pace for long periods of time.

As Ederle entered the water, she was joined by a support staff on a boat that would follow her during the swim. This crew included her coach, Thomas Burgess, who was also a Channel swimmer, as well as additional supporters who offered navigation, sustenance, and emotional support. Margaret, Ederle's sister, was also on board and served as a key emotional anchor. The support staff was critical not only in guaranteeing Ederle's safety, but also in sustaining her morale throughout the arduous trek.

The English Channel, also known as the "Mount Everest of swimming," faced various hurdles. The water temperature hovered around 60 degrees Fahrenheit, chilly enough to sap the vigor of even the most powerful swimmer. The currents were unpredictable, driving swimmers off course and adding additional distance to their swim. Furthermore, the salty water caused persistent irritation, especially to the eyes and throat. Despite these hurdles, Ederle stayed focused, motivated by a strong desire to achieve.

Ederle began her swim in Cape Gris-Nez, the closest point on the French coast to England. Her objective was to swim in a straight path to Dover, which was hindered by the changing tides and currents. Ederle's coach and support staff communicated with her through a system of signals that indicated if she needed to change course. This communication was critical because visibility in the water was limited, and Ederle frequently relied on her team's advice rather than sight.

As the hours passed, Ederle faced several hurdles. The waves grew larger, and the wind increased, making swimming more difficult. At times, she had to swim against strong currents, which slowed her pace and sapped her stamina. Despite the hurdles, Ederle kept a steady stroke, her desire unshakeable. She employed a crawl stroke, which was faster than the breaststroke used by earlier swimmers but needed more effort. This decision paid off because it allowed her to cover more ground faster, despite the difficult conditions.

The mental struggle proved to be one of the most challenging components of the swim. The monotony of the endless water, mixed with physical exhaustion and cold, could quickly lead to despair. However, Ederle shown great mental fortitude. She sung to herself, recited poetry, and concentrated on the rhythm of her strokes to keep her mind busy. Her sister, Margaret, also performed an important role, delivering words of encouragement and support from the boat. Ederle's coach attempted to remove her from the water once, afraid for her safety. Ederle famously replied, "What for?" expressing her desire to persevere regardless of the challenge.

As Ederle approached the English coast, the weather grew increasingly difficult. The currents grew stronger, pulling her off track and forcing her to swim further than expected. Ederle's crew estimates that she swam about 35 miles, which is far more than the 21-mile straight line distance between France and England. Despite the physical and mental toll, Ederle persevered, motivated by the awareness that she was about to make history. Her determination was evident, demonstrating her strength and will.

Ederle arrived at Kingsdown near Dover, England, after 14 hours and 34 minutes on the water. Exhausted but triumphant, she was dragged from the water by her teammates and quickly engulfed by a crowd of screaming fans. Ederle not only became the first woman to swim the English Channel, but she also broke the current record, exceeding the previous men's time by nearly two hours. Her accomplishment was a breathtaking display of physical endurance, mental fortitude, and the strength of human determination.

Ederle's spectacular swim was more than just a personal achievement; it was a watershed moment for women's athletics. At a time when conventional expectations limited women's roles and prospects, Ederle's success defied prejudices and revealed that women could perform incredible physical feats. Her achievement encouraged countless women to pursue their own athletic goals, paving the door for greater gender equality in sports.

Ederle's swim received widespread media coverage in the United States and around the world. Newspapers lauded her as a hero, and her achievements were commemorated with parades and awards. Ederle became an instant celebrity, earning recognition from all around the world. Despite her newfound celebrity, Ederle remained humble, crediting her accomplishment to hard work, perseverance, and the support of her teammates and family.

In the years that followed her historic swim, Ederle remained active in the sports world, promoting swimming and fighting for female athletics. She also encountered personal problems, such as a significant injury that restricted her ability to participate. Despite these losses, Ederle's legacy lives on, not only as a record-breaking swimmer, but also as a trailblazer who increased women's opportunities in athletics and beyond.

Ederle's experience, summarized in the title "Young Woman and the Sea," exemplifies the strength of determination and the importance of shattering obstacles. Her swim across the English Channel is still remembered as a legendary feat in sports history, representing the courage and resilience required to overcome apparently impossible obstacles. Ederle's legacy continues to inspire future generations of athletes, serving as a reminder of our own infinite potential.

Chapter Four

Breaking Barriers and Legacy

Gertrude Ederle's effort to become the first woman to swim across the English Channel was more than just a personal victory; it was a watershed moment in the history of sports and gender equality. Her accomplishment demolished the widespread belief that women were physically inferior and incapable of facing the same physical demands as men. In the 1920s, a time of great social change and the struggle for women's rights, Ederle's accomplishment became a potent emblem of female empowerment and resilience.

At the time, men dominated the world of athletics, and women were frequently barred from participating in major athletic competitions. It was practically inconceivable for a woman to compete in such a rigorous activity as long-distance swimming. Gertrude Ederle, with her unwavering dedication and tenacity, challenged these antiquated beliefs. Her achievement not only established a new world record, but also changed what women could accomplish in sports.

The English Channel, with its hazardous waters and unpredictable weather, had proven to be a tough obstacle for even the most experienced male swimmers. Before Ederle's successful effort, only five men had made the crossing. Many people believed that a woman could never accomplish this accomplishment. Nonetheless, Ederle's confidence and unwavering spirit propelled her to not only complete the swim, but do so faster than any man before her, finishing in 14 hours and 34 minutes. This astounding performance astonished the globe and spurred a reevaluation of women's athletic ability.

Ederle's accomplishment was more than just setting a world record; it was also about shattering barriers. Her success occurred at a time when the feminist movement was gaining traction, and her accomplishment became a forceful statement for women's rights. She demonstrated that women could compete on the same level as men, motivating numerous women and girls to pursue their own aspirations, whether in sports or other industries.

Ederle's success had far-reaching consequences beyond the sport of swimming. She became a national hero in the United States, and her name was hailed around the world. Newspapers referred to her as the "Queen of the Waves," and President Calvin Coolidge invited her to the White House, calling her "America's best girl." Her accomplishment was more than simply a personal one; it was a win for all women, demonstrating that gender should not be an impediment to excellence.

The changes that occurred as a result of Ederle's accomplishment reflect her legacy as well. Her swim across the English Channel paved the way for women in competitive sports, providing more chances and recognition for female athletes. Prior to her historic swim, women had restricted access to competitive events, and their accomplishments were frequently dismissed or overlooked. Ederle's accomplishment shattered these expectations and paved the way for subsequent generations of female athletes.

Furthermore, Ederle's story appealed to a wider audience, transcending the realm of sports. She became a symbol of tenacity and courage, inspiring people from all walks of life. Her journey was not without difficulties; she received criticism and distrust from those who questioned her ability. Nevertheless, she persisted, motivated by her passion and determination. Her narrative demonstrates the strength of perseverance and the value of believing in oneself, especially in the face of hardship.

In the years after her remarkable swim, Ederle continued to inspire and impact others. She became an advocate for swimming and water safety, especially among women and children. She taught swimming and encouraged young females to participate in the sport, emphasizing the value of physical fitness and self-esteem. Her efforts helped to increase women's acceptance and support in athletics, leaving a legacy that lives on today.

Gertrude Ederle's impact can still be seen in athletics and other fields. Her innovative feat shook traditional norms and broadened women's opportunities. She demonstrated that with persistence and hard effort, obstacles could be overcome and new paths formed. Her story is more than just an athletic accomplishment; it is about courage, resilience, and the desire of equality.

As we consider Ederle's legacy, it is critical to remember the larger environment in which she completed her historic swim. The 1920s were a period of great social and cultural upheaval, particularly for women. The suffrage movement had recently won a huge success with the ratification of the 19th Amendment, which gave women the right to vote. Gender discrimination persisted, and women continued to battle for equal opportunity in many spheres of life, including sports.

Ederle's accomplishment provided hope to others who advocated for gender equality. It gave practical proof that women could thrive in the same fields as men. Her tale was widely covered by the media, and she became a role model for women and girls all around the country. The public recognition of her accomplishment signaled a shift in attitudes about women in athletics, paving the path for increased acceptance and support.

In the decades since, the obstacles that Ederle helped to remove have continued to crumble. Women's participation in competitive sports increased, and their successes began to be recognized. Organizations such as the Women's Sports Foundation and Title IX legislation contributed to the cause of gender equality in sports, guaranteeing that future generations of female athletes may compete on a level playing field. Ederle's legacy is an important part of our history, and her narrative continues to inspire and motivate.

Gertrude Ederle's impact goes on today, not only in the swimming world, but also in the larger campaign for gender equality. Her success serves as a reminder of the value of perseverance, determination, and fortitude in the face of adversity. She demonstrated to the world that women could achieve greatness and that their accomplishments deserved to be recognized and honored.

To summarize, Gertrude Ederle's swim across the English Channel was more than just an incredible athletic performance; it was a watershed moment in the history of women's sports and a forceful statement about women's possibilities. Her legacy continues to inspire and motivate us to break down barriers and work toward equality. As we reflect on her extraordinary journey, we celebrate not only her accomplishment, but also the progress that has been done since then and the work that remains. Ederle's narrative demonstrates the power of dreams, the value of tenacity, and the lasting impact of people who dare to defy the existing quo.

Chapter Five

The Movie Adaptation: "Young Woman and the Sea

For decades, audiences have been enthralled by the actual story of Gertrude Ederle, famously recognized as the first woman to swim the English Channel. Her extraordinary journey, marked by persistence, fortitude, and breaking cultural barriers, is beautifully shown in the film adaptation "Young Woman and the Sea." This film sheds light on the life and legacy of a woman who beat the odds and established new standards for sports, particularly women, in the early twentieth century.

"Young Woman and the Sea" looks about Gertrude Ederle's life, from her impoverished beginnings to her historic swim on August 6, 1926. The video captures the essence of Ederle's character, portraying her as a young woman full of enthusiasm and a never-ending ambition to do what many thought was impossible. The casting and direction decisions are critical in conveying Ederle's journey with honesty and emotional depth.

The film opens by focusing on Ederle's upbringing in New York City as a German immigrant. Her introduction to swimming, a sport she rapidly excelled at, is shown with nostalgia and admiration. The filmmakers take care to reflect societal standards at the period, particularly the constraints put on women in athletics. This backdrop is critical for comprehending the significance of Ederle's accomplishments, as she aspired not only to overcome a severe physical task but also to challenge gender stereotypes.

As the story develops, the video digs into Ederle's intense training regimen, as well as the physical and psychological hurdles she endured. Her training is meticulously depicted, highlighting the many hours spent in the water, the dietary regimen, and the mental strength required to complete such a difficult endeavor. The viewer is made to feel her training's intensity, the chilly water of the English Channel, and the strong currents that may dissuade even the most experienced swimmers. The film does a good job of depicting these problems not only as physical impediments, but also as analogies for the societal boundaries that Ederle was determined to conquer.

The day of the historic swim is a turning point in the film, shown with a mix of stress and elation. The filmmakers expertly build up to this moment, displaying Ederle's popular and media backing and doubt, respectively. The involvement of her support network, notably her coach and sister, is highlighted, demonstrating the group effort and emotional investment in her endeavour. The actual swim is shown with dramatic flair, depicting the unexpected weather conditions, the physical toll on Ederle, and her unwavering will. The sequences are designed to emphasize the gravity of her undertaking, as well as the personal and physical risks involved.

One of the film's most dramatic scenes depicts Ederle's perseverance and resilience. The tale does not shy away from depicting Ederle's periods of doubt, exhaustion, and near despair while swimming. These scenes play an important role in humanizing her character, depicting her as a sympathetic young woman with anxieties and flaws rather than merely a sporting star. The video successfully contrasts these images with shots of Ederle gathering strength from her supporters, her training, and her own inner power. The presentation is motivating, emphasizing the concept that true courage is not the absence of fear, but rather the desire to overcome it.

The film also delves into the consequences of Ederle's unprecedented achievement. Her victorious landing on the borders of France is presented with joy, conveying the global fame and admiration she received. However, the film does not conclude on a high note. It delves into the nuances of Ederle's life after swimming, such as the trials of fame, her struggles with hearing loss, and her role as a trailblazer for women in athletics. The story explores the bittersweet character of her legacy, noting both her remarkable success and the emotional sacrifices she made.

"Young Woman and the Sea" is more than just a tale of physical success; it is also a profound examination of a young woman's struggle for recognition and acceptance. The video goes at the sociological implications of Ederle's accomplishment, notably how it challenged and altered notions of women's ability in sports and beyond. The filmmakers made an intentional attempt to demonstrate how Ederle became a symbol of female empowerment, inspiring future generations. The film captures the essence of her legacy, depicting her not only as a sports pioneer, but also as a steadfast figure in the struggle for gender equality.

The film's photography and musical composition greatly enhance its emotional and inspirational impact. The graphics, particularly the broad panoramas of the ocean and the harsh conditions of the Channel, are both stunning and terrifying, highlighting the enormity of Ederle's endeavor. The music enhances these scenes, with a score that goes from tight and frightening during the swim to uplifting and triumphant during moments of victory. These aspects combine to produce an immersive experience, engulfing the spectator in Ederle's trip and the emotions that accompany it.

Finally, "Young Woman and the Sea" is a gripping picture of Gertrude Ederle's life and famous swim across the English Channel. The film effectively conveys the spirit of her character, the obstacles she encountered, and the greater social consequences of her accomplishments. It is a narrative of bravery, tenacity, and breaking down boundaries, portrayed with delicacy and respect for the real-life events and characters involved. The film not only honors Ederle's legacy, but also serves as a reminder of the force of endurance and the significance of questioning conventional standards. This film voyage inspires viewers to consider their own obstacles and the opportunity to overcome them, much as Ederle did nearly a century ago.

Chapter Six

Conclusion

On August 6, 1926, Gertrude Ederle swam the final strokes to the shore of Kingsdown, England, completing a historic journey across the English Channel; she etched her name into history, not just as a champion swimmer, but also as a symbol of resilience and the breaking down of societal barriers. Her achievement was a triumph not only of athleticism but also of spirit, symbolizing a significant shift in perceptions of women's ability in sports and beyond.

Gertrude's quest was more than just crossing a body of water; it was about challenging the existing quo and demonstrating that persistence and courage can conquer even the most difficult challenges. The English Channel, also known as the "Mount Everest" of swimming, presented severe hurdles. The very cold seas, powerful currents, and unpredictable weather made it a difficult task for any swimmer, regardless of gender. Nonetheless, Ederle rose to the occasion, setting a new world record time of 14 hours and 34 minutes, thanks to her unwavering determination and meticulous preparation. This accomplishment was not only a personal triumph, but a watershed event for women everywhere.

Following her swim, Ederle became an international phenomenon. Her accomplishment was heralded in newspapers all around the world, and she was dubbed "Queen of the

Waves" and "America's Best Girl." However, the significance of her feat extended beyond the praises and headlines. It was a bold statement against the existing gender standards of the period, which frequently put women to the background in athletics and other public venues. Ederle's accomplishment revealed that women can achieve greatness in traditionally male-dominated areas, upsetting conventional expectations and motivating numerous others to pursue their passions regardless of gender.

The impact of Ederle's swim extended far beyond the realm of sports. It sparked a shift in how women were regarded in society, prompting a reassessment of women's responsibilities and capacities. In the 1920s, women were still fighting for their rights and recognition in a variety of areas, including the opportunity to vote, work, and play sports. Ederle's triumph was a beacon of promise, demonstrating that women could flourish in fields traditionally assumed to be exclusively male. This was especially important in the context of the suffrage movement and the larger struggle for women's rights, as it demonstrated women's strength, dedication, and potential.

In the years since her swim, Ederle has continued to inspire as a motivational speaker and fitness advocate. Her narrative demonstrated the strength of tenacity and the value of pushing one's boundaries. Despite her fame and notoriety, Ederle remained humble and focused on inspiring others, particularly young women, to achieve their aspirations and believe in themselves. Her impact was not only as a spectacular athlete, but also as a role model who exemplified the characteristics of courage, tenacity, and resilience.

Gertrude Ederle's narrative was memorialized in a variety of media, including novels, documentaries, and, most notably, the film "Young Woman and the Sea." The film adaptation shared her extraordinary adventure with a new generation, reflecting the enthusiasm and determination that distinguished her life. The film depicted Ederle's physical obstacles as well as her emotional and psychological struggles, using vivid storytelling and powerful performances. It gave an intimate glimpse into her personality, her unwavering determination, and the support network that helped her achieve her goals. The video was more than just a celebration of Ederle's historic swim; it told a larger story about shattering barriers and confronting society standards.

Ederle's legacy lives on, not only as a swimming pioneer, but also as a symbol of the larger struggle for gender equality and acknowledgment. Her feat paved the path for future generations of female athletes and adventurers, motivating women to pursue their dreams without fear. She demonstrated that exceptional results can be achieved with hard work, devotion, and an unwillingness to accept constraints. Her narrative still resonates today, reminding us of the value of pushing above cultural bounds and aiming for perfection.

When reflecting on Gertrude Ederle's life and accomplishments, it is critical to consider the larger context of her success. The 1920s were a period of enormous social change, and Ederle's swim both reflected and accelerated these developments. It questioned traditional conceptions of femininity and athleticism, urging a reconsideration of what women could accomplish. It also emphasized the value of visibility and representation in sports, demonstrating how women's participation in high-profile athletic undertakings can inspire and empower others.

Gertrude Ederle's story is more than simply a historical footnote; it continues to inspire others who confront apparently insurmountable problems. Her legacy lives on via the numerous women who have followed in her footsteps, shattering records and setting new standards in sports and other industries. It serves as a reminder that true greatness is the bravery to face the impossible and the perseverance to see it through.

In conclusion, Gertrude Ederle's triumphant swim across the English Channel was a watershed moment that transcended sports. It was a powerful statement about women's capabilities and the significance of questioning traditional standards. Her legacy is one of inspiration and strength, demonstrating the power of tenacity and the importance of breaking down obstacles. As we reflect on her extraordinary life and accomplishments, we are reminded of the value of courage, persistence, and unflinching faith in one's ability to influence history.

Milton Keynes UK
Ingram Content Group UK Ltd.
UKHW021348160924
1675UKWH00077B/1230

9 798330 315109